HOW TO W
BIG TRUCKS

Mark Bergin

BOOK HOUSE

SALARIYA

Published in Great Britain in 2008 by
Book House, an imprint of
The Salariya Book Company Ltd
25 Marlborough Place, Brighton BN1 1UB

3 5 7 9 8 6 4 2

Please visit our website at **www.salariya.com**
for **free** electronic versions of:
You Wouldn't Want to Be an Egyptian Mummy!
You Wouldn't Want to Be a Roman Gladiator!
Avoid Joining Shackleton's Polar Expedition!
Avoid Sailing on a 19th-Century Whaling Ship!

Author: Mark Bergin was born in Hastings in 1961. He
studied at Eastbourne College of Art and has specialised
in historical reconstructions as well as aviation and
maritime subjects since 1983. He lives in Bexhill-on-
Sea with his wife and three children.

Editors: Rob Walker, Stephen Haynes

PB ISBN: 978-1-906370-33-6

A CIP catalogue record for this
book is available from the
British Library.

Printed and bound in China.
Printed on paper from
sustainable sources.
Reprinted in 2009.

PAPER FROM
SUSTAINABLE
FORESTS

Contents

4   Making a start

6   Perspective

8   Photographs

10   Drawing materials

12   Sketching

14   Simple views

16   Fire engine

18   Articulated truck

20   Racing truck

22   Snow plough

24   Tanker

26   Future truck

28   Giant dump truck

30   Monster truck

32   Glossary and Index

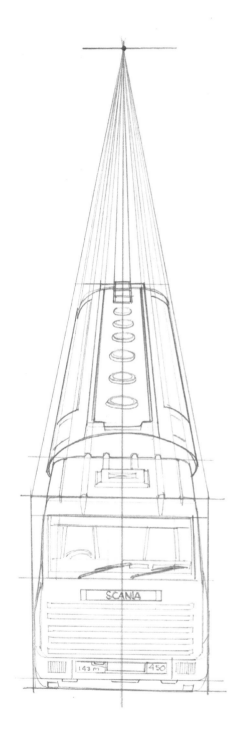

Making a start

Learning to draw is about looking and seeing. Keep practising, and get to know your subject. Use a sketchbook to make quick drawings. Start by doodling, and experiment with shapes and patterns. There are many ways to draw; this book shows one method. Visit art galleries, look at artists' drawings, see how friends draw, but above all, find your own way.

Fine-line pen

Felt-tip pens

Remember that practice makes perfect. If it looks wrong, start again. Keep working at it — the more you draw, the more you will learn.

Ballpoint pen

Pencil

Perspective

If you look at any object from different viewpoints, you will see that the part that is closest to you looks larger, and the part furthest away from you looks smaller. Drawing in perspective is a way of creating a feeling of depth — of showing three dimensions on a flat surface.

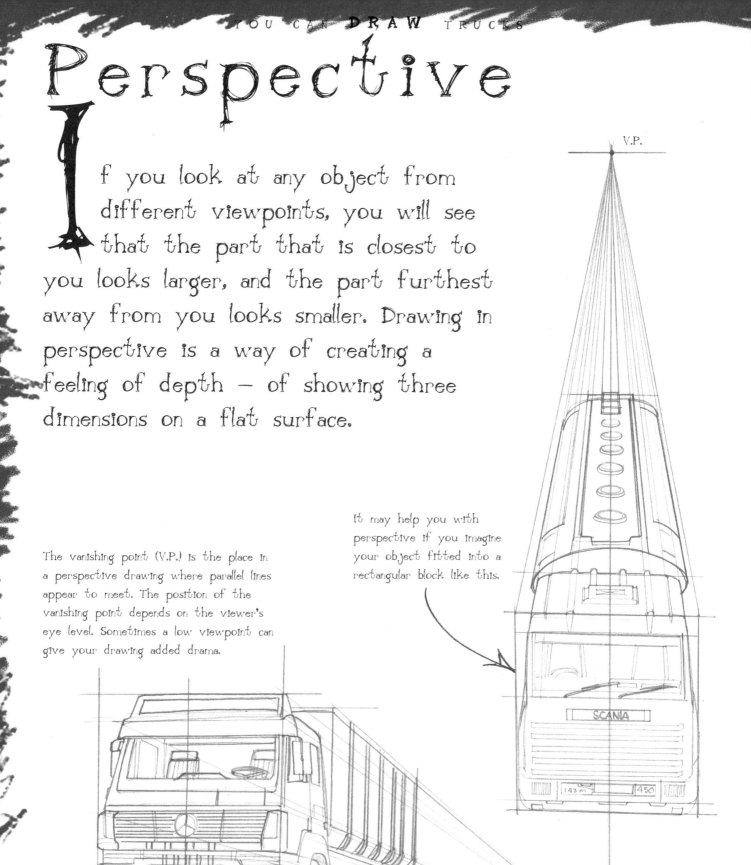

The vanishing point (V.P.) is the place in a perspective drawing where parallel lines appear to meet. The position of the vanishing point depends on the viewer's eye level. Sometimes a low viewpoint can give your drawing added drama.

It may help you with perspective if you imagine your object fitted into a rectangular block like this.

V.P.

SCANIA

143 m   450

V.P.

Two-point perspective drawing

Two-point perspective uses two vanishing points: one for lines running along the length of the object, and one on the opposite side for lines running across the width of the object.

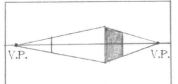

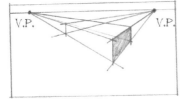

V.P.   V.P.

Normal eye level.

In these drawings the vanishing points are outside the picture.

High eye level
(view from above)

V.P.   V.P.

Three-point perspective uses a third vanishing point for lines running vertically up or down. This gives a very realistic three-dimensional effect.

Overhead eye level
(view looking down)

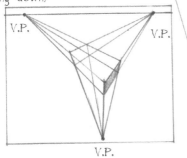

V.P.   V.P.

V.P.

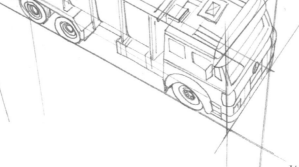

V.P. = vanishing point

7

Photographs

Drawing from photographs can help you practise your drawing skills. It is important that you consider the position of your drawing on the paper; this is part of what is meant by 'composition'.

First make a tracing of the photograph.

Then lightly draw a squared grid over your traced image.

Grids

Enlarging a drawing by using a grid of squares to guide you is called 'squaring up'.

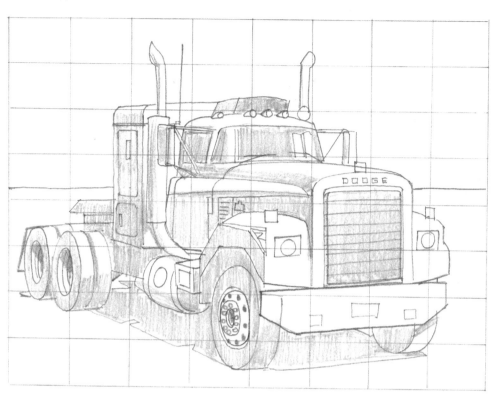

Lightly draw another grid on your drawing paper, using larger squares than before but keeping the same proportions. You can now copy the shapes in each square of your tracing grid onto your drawing grid.

Add more tone and detail to finish the drawing.

By adding a background you can give much more atmosphere to your finished drawing.

Drawing materials

Try using different types of drawing papers and materials. Experiment with charcoal, wax crayons and pastels. All pens, from felt-tips to ballpoints, will make interesting marks — or try drawing with pen and ink on wet paper.

Hard **pencils** are greyer and soft pencils are blacker. Hard pencils are graded from 6H (the hardest) through 5H, 4H, 3H and 2H to H. Soft pencils are graded from B, 2B, 3B, 4B and 5B up to 6B (the softest).

Charcoal is very soft and can be used for big, bold drawings. Ask an adult to spray your charcoal drawings with fixative to prevent smudging.

Silhouette is a style of drawing that uses only a solid black shadow.

Pastels are even softer than charcoal, and come in a wide range of colours. Ask an adult to spray your pastel drawings with fixative to prevent smudging.

You can create special effects by scraping away parts of a drawing done with **wax crayons.**

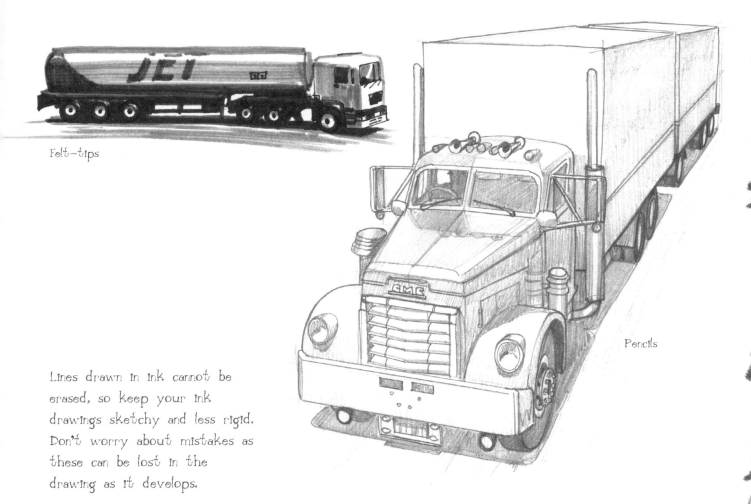

Felt-tips

Pencils

Lines drawn in ink cannot be
erased, so keep your ink
drawings sketchy and less rigid.
Don't worry about mistakes as
these can be lost in the
drawing as it develops.

Pen and ink

Sketching

You can't always rely on your memory, so you have to look around and find real—life things you want to draw. Using a sketchbook is one of the best ways to build up drawing skills. Learn to observe objects: see how they move, how they are made and how they work. You should try to draw what you have seen. Since the 15th century, artists have used sketchbooks to record their ideas and drawings.

Sketching models

Try drawing model trucks. It is good practice for seeing and observing the general shapes.

Sketching

A quick sketch can often catch
as much information as a careful
drawing that has taken many
hours of patient work.

13

Simple views

Drawing a simple side or front view of a truck first can help you when it comes to three–dimensional drawing.

Start drawing the truck in the side view using simple squares, rectangles and circles.

Add more straight lines to divide the truck into its basic shapes.

Now add the major details of the truck.

Finish the drawing by adding more detail and some shading.

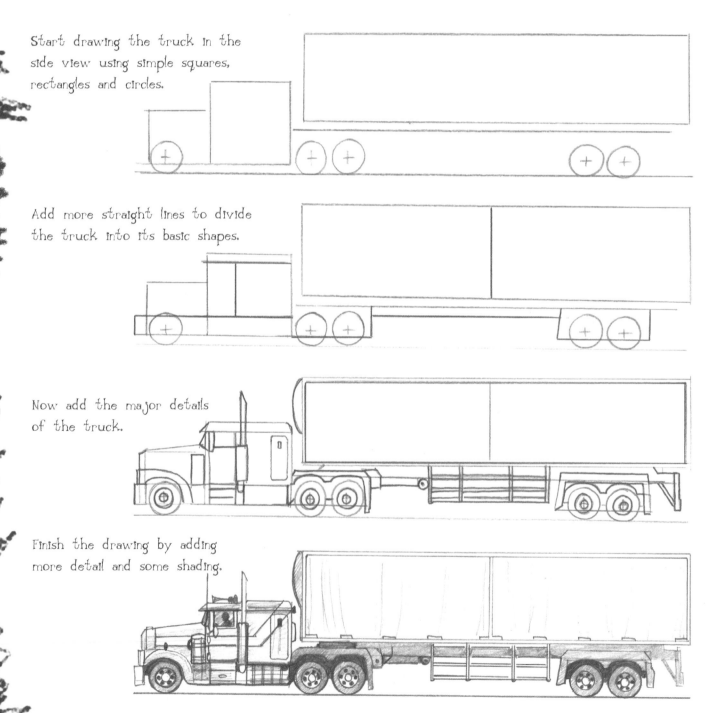

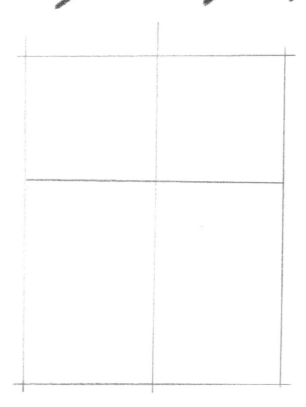

Draw a box. Divide it in two vertically. Draw in a horizontal line above centre.

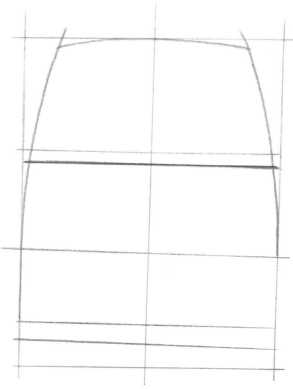

Add further horizontal lines as shown, and curved lines at the top corners.

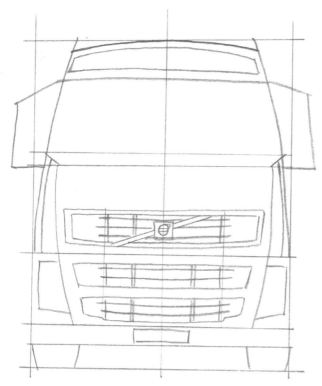

Draw in the shapes of the main details of the truck.

Complete your drawing by finishing all the details. Shade areas as shown. Erase any unwanted construction lines.

Fire engine

A fire engine is designed to pump water mechanically, using a powerful engine. This American fire truck has an extendable ladder on a turntable.

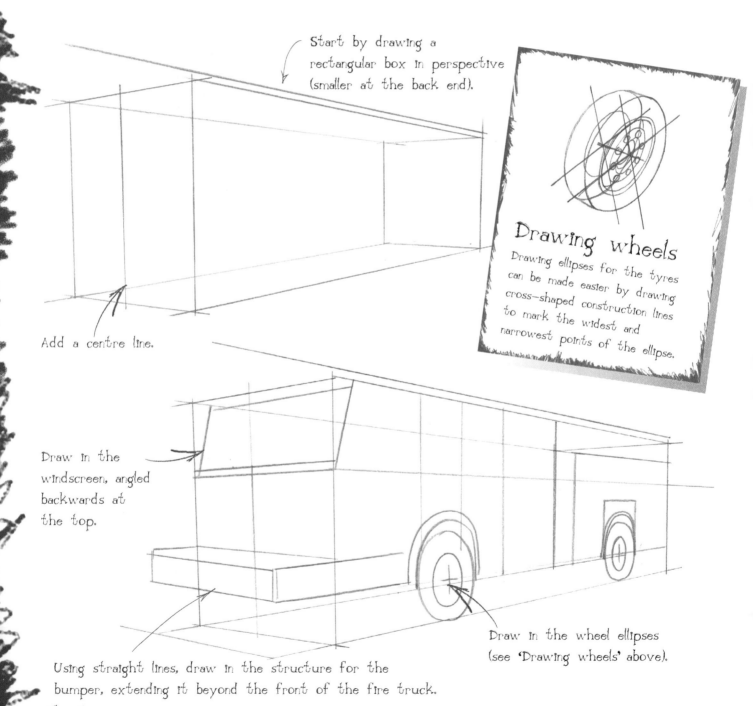

Start by drawing a rectangular box in perspective (smaller at the back end).

Add a centre line.

Drawing wheels

Drawing ellipses for the tyres can be made easier by drawing cross-shaped construction lines to mark the widest and narrowest points of the ellipse.

Draw in the windscreen, angled backwards at the top.

Draw in the wheel ellipses (see 'Drawing wheels' above).

Using straight lines, draw in the structure for the bumper, extending it beyond the front of the fire truck.

For the ladder, draw a long box in perspective on top of the fire truck. It extends beyond the front bumper and stops short of the rear of the truck. Draw in the details of the ladder.

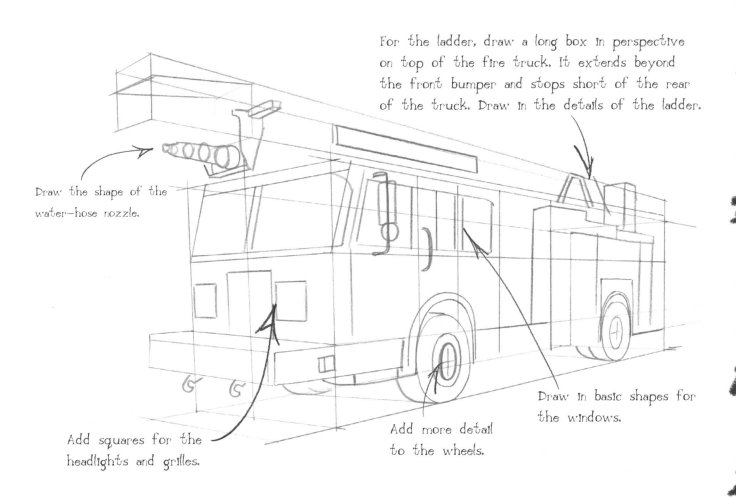

Draw the shape of the water-hose nozzle.

Add squares for the headlights and grilles.

Add more detail to the wheels.

Draw in basic shapes for the windows.

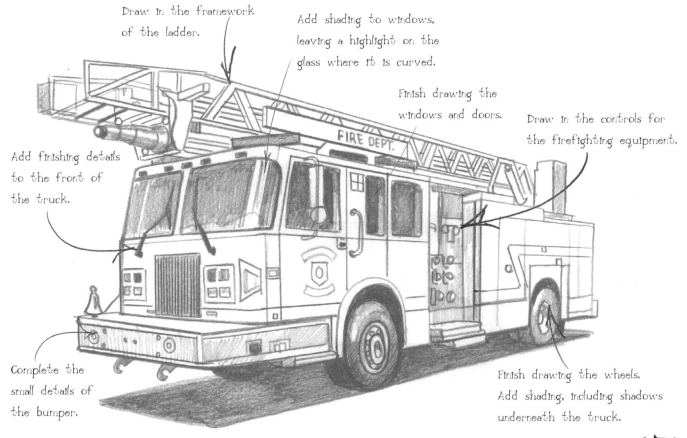

Draw in the framework of the ladder.

Add shading to windows, leaving a highlight on the glass where it is curved.

Finish drawing the windows and doors.

Draw in the controls for the firefighting equipment.

Add finishing details to the front of the truck.

FIRE DEPT.

Complete the small details of the bumper.

Finish drawing the wheels. Add shading, including shadows underneath the truck.

Articulated truck

This typically American articulated truck is very powerful and can pull many different types of trailer. The truck also has a large cab in which the driver can sleep.

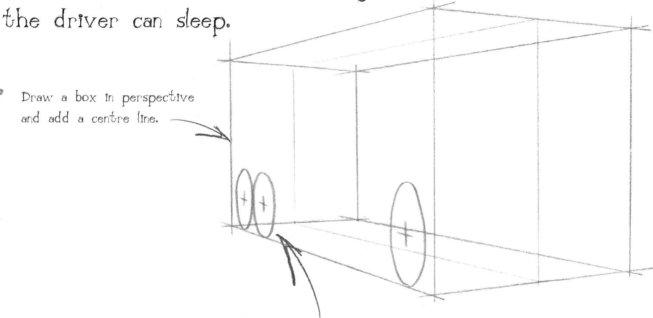

Draw a box in perspective and add a centre line.

Draw in the wheel ellipses.

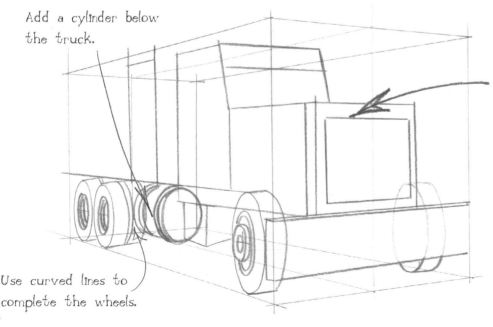

Add a cylinder below the truck.

Using your original box as a guide, start to draw in the recessed shape of the truck using straight lines.

Use curved lines to complete the wheels.

18

Add a large exhaust pipe on either side of the cab.

Draw in the windows.

Add circles for the headlights.

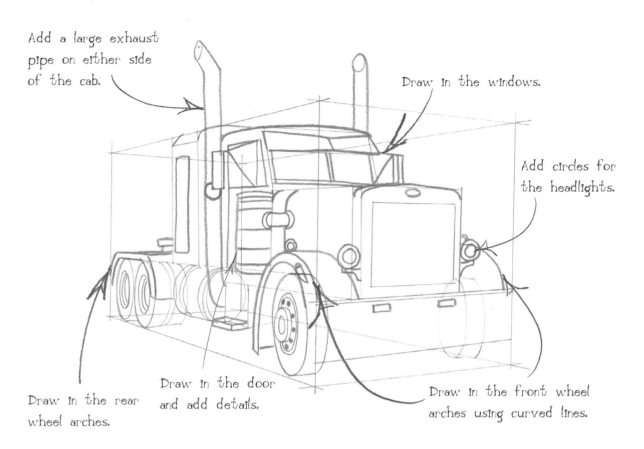

Draw in the rear wheel arches.

Draw in the door and add details.

Draw in the front wheel arches using curved lines.

Add shading to one side of the exhaust pipes.

Finish the detail on the windows.

Using straight lines and heavy shading, draw in the front grille.

Add the details to the cab.

Complete small details such as the headlights.

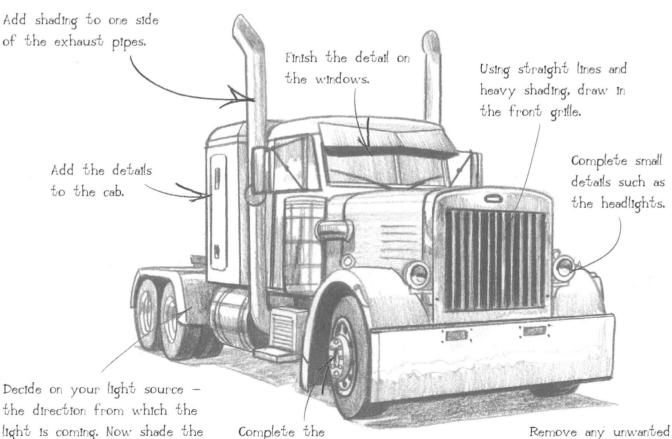

Decide on your light source — the direction from which the light is coming. Now shade the areas that face away from the light source.

Complete the wheel details.

Remove any unwanted construction lines.

19

Racing truck

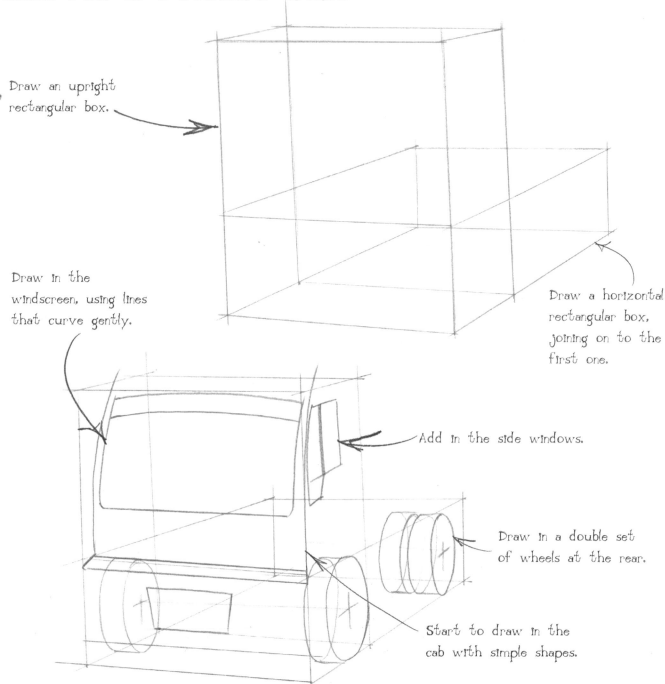

A racing truck can be tuned up to 1,300 brake horsepower. It uses four times as much diesel fuel as a standard truck.

Draw an upright rectangular box.

Draw a horizontal rectangular box, joining on to the first one.

Draw in the windscreen, using lines that curve gently.

Add in the side windows.

Draw in a double set of wheels at the rear.

Start to draw in the cab with simple shapes.

Sketch in the driver.

Draw in straight lines to mark out the shape of the chassis.

Add the wheel arches.

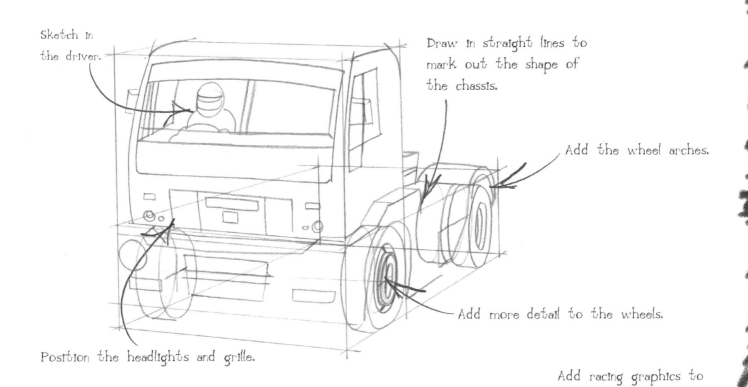

Add more detail to the wheels.

Position the headlights and grille.

Add racing graphics to the side of the truck.

Darken the inside of the cab, highlighting the driver.

Composition
Framing your drawing with a square or rectangle can make it look completely different.

Complete the details on the side of the truck.

Complete the details on the front of the truck, including graphics.

Add in the kerb of the racetrack.

Shade areas that face away from the light source.

Remove any unwanted construction lines.

Snow plough

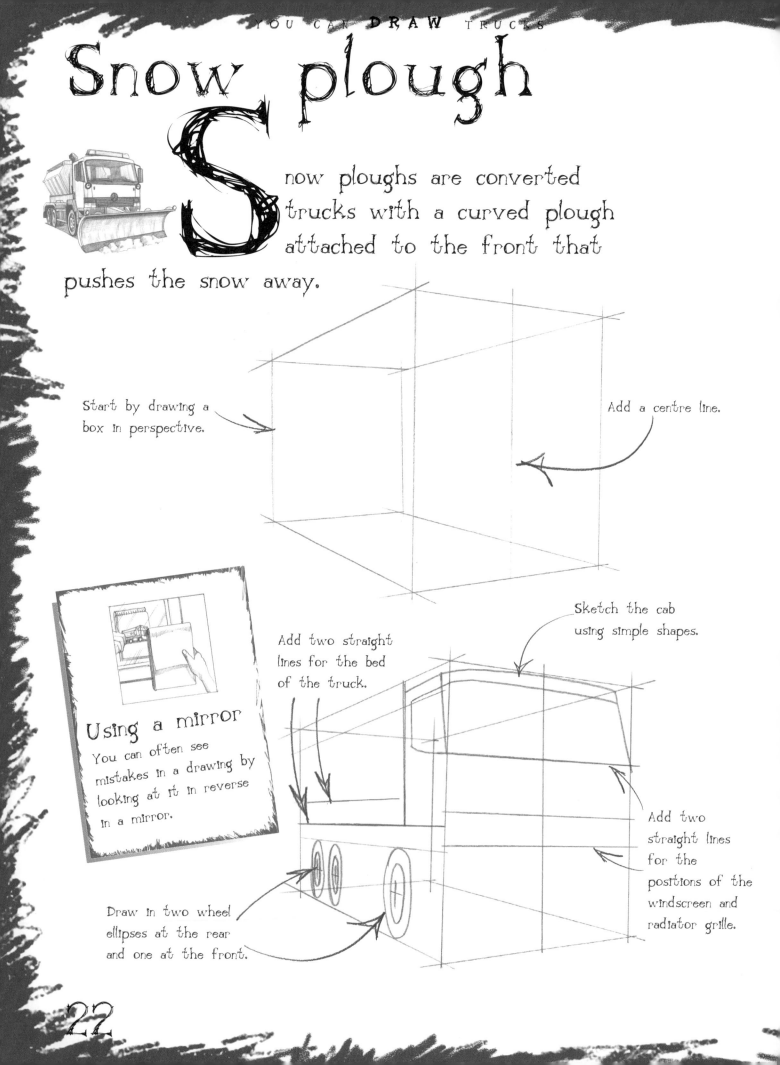

Snow ploughs are converted trucks with a curved plough attached to the front that pushes the snow away.

Start by drawing a box in perspective.

Add a centre line.

Using a mirror

You can often see mistakes in a drawing by looking at it in reverse in a mirror.

Add two straight lines for the bed of the truck.

Sketch the cab using simple shapes.

Add two straight lines for the positions of the windscreen and radiator grille.

Draw in two wheel ellipses at the rear and one at the front.

Draw in the metal container at the rear of the truck using your construction lines as a guide.

Sketch in the exhaust pipe.

Sketch in the wing mirrors.

Add basic details to the front: badge, grille, headlights, etc.

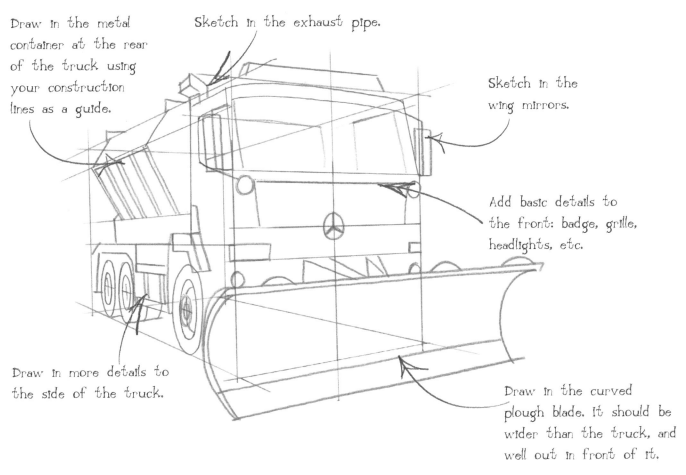

Draw in more details to the side of the truck.

Draw in the curved plough blade. It should be wider than the truck, and well out in front of it.

Add shading to the windows to show the shapes inside the cab.

Add shading to areas where the light source would not reach.

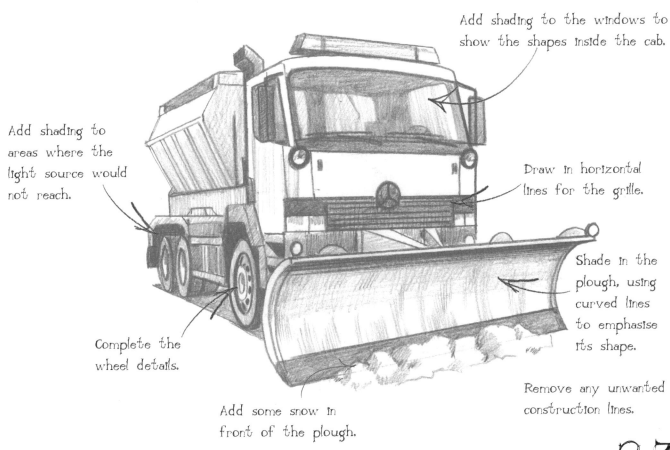

Draw in horizontal lines for the grille.

Shade in the plough, using curved lines to emphasise its shape.

Complete the wheel details.

Add some snow in front of the plough.

Remove any unwanted construction lines.

23

Tanker

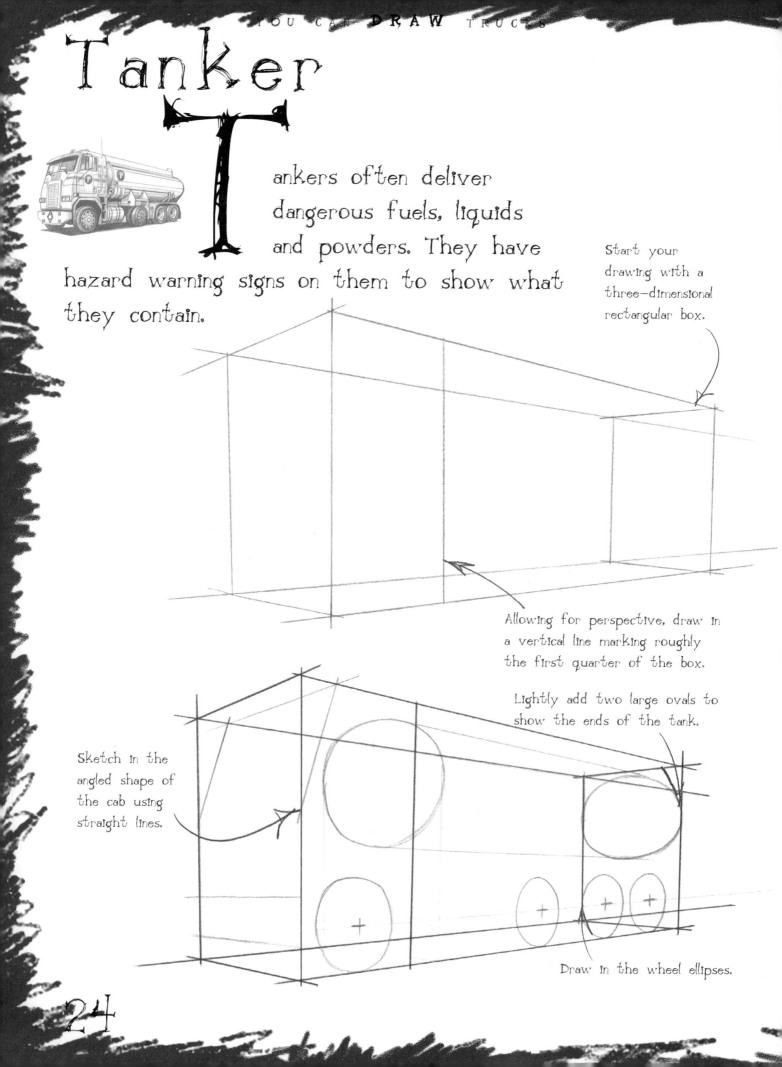

Tankers often deliver dangerous fuels, liquids and powders. They have hazard warning signs on them to show what they contain.

Start your drawing with a three-dimensional rectangular box.

Allowing for perspective, draw in a vertical line marking roughly the first quarter of the box.

Lightly add two large ovals to show the ends of the tank.

Sketch in the angled shape of the cab using straight lines.

Draw in the wheel ellipses.

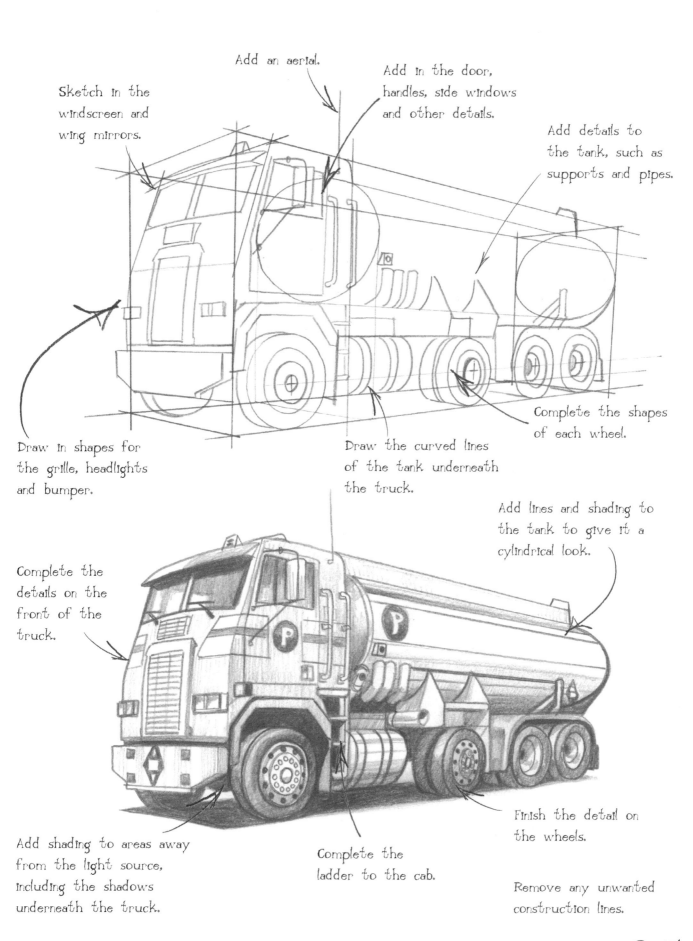

Add an aerial.

Sketch in the windscreen and wing mirrors.

Add in the door, handles, side windows and other details.

Add details to the tank, such as supports and pipes.

Draw in shapes for the grille, headlights and bumper.

Draw the curved lines of the tank underneath the truck.

Complete the shapes of each wheel.

Add lines and shading to the tank to give it a cylindrical look.

Complete the details on the front of the truck.

Add shading to areas away from the light source, including the shadows underneath the truck.

Complete the ladder to the cab.

Finish the detail on the wheels.

Remove any unwanted construction lines.

25

Future truck

The Renault truck 'Radiance' is highly streamlined to create less wind resistance. As well as rear—view mirrors it has monitors inside the driver's cab.

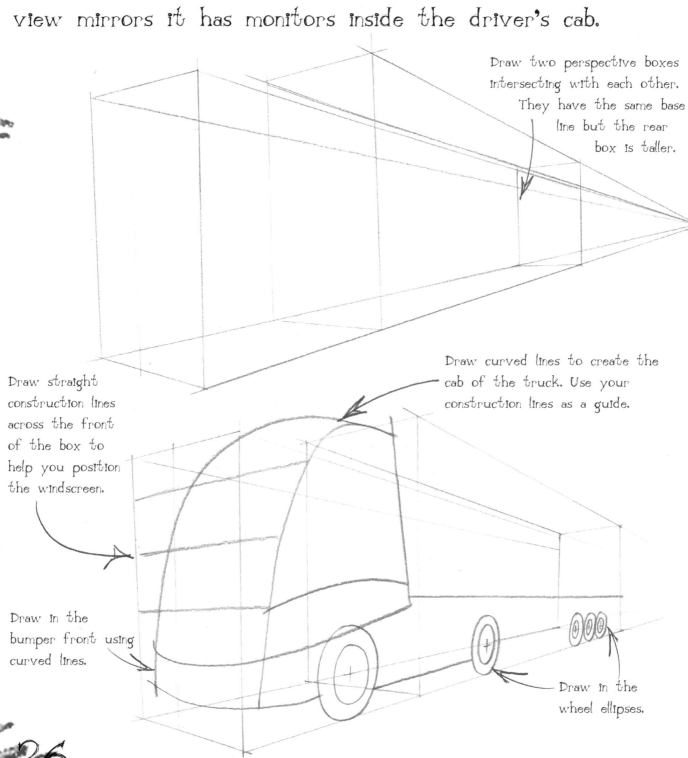

Draw two perspective boxes intersecting with each other. They have the same base line but the rear box is taller.

Draw straight construction lines across the front of the box to help you position the windscreen.

Draw curved lines to create the cab of the truck. Use your construction lines as a guide.

Draw in the bumper front using curved lines.

Draw in the wheel ellipses.

Carefully position and draw in the windscreen.

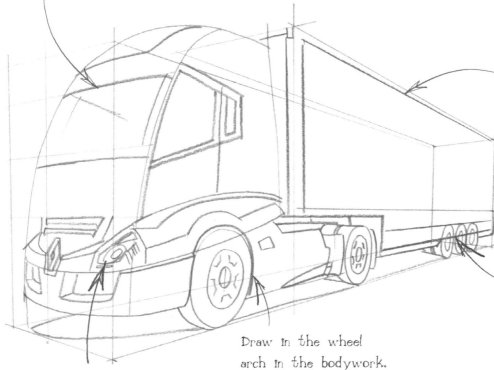

Draw in the box-shaped trailer using straight lines.

Add more detail to the wheels; note that they are partially covered.

Draw in the wheel arch in the bodywork.

Add the headlights and other details.

Use different tones of shading for the windscreen and the inside of the cab.

Add the driver.

Add shading to the side of the trailer.

Add shading on the front.

Add shading to areas that face away from the light.

Complete the small details on the wheels.

Remove any unwanted construction lines.

27

Giant dump truck

These huge dump trucks work in opencast mines and quarries. They can carry 45 tonnes of rocks and dirt.

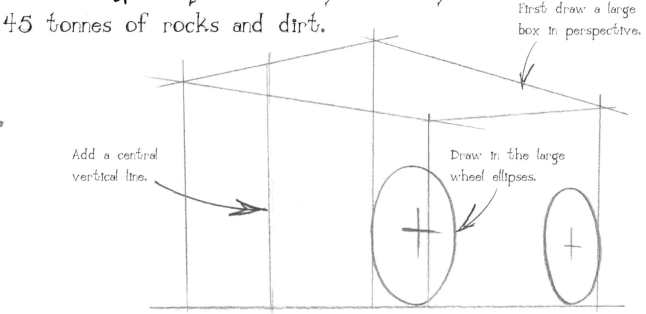

First draw a large box in perspective.

Add a central vertical line.

Draw in the large wheel ellipses.

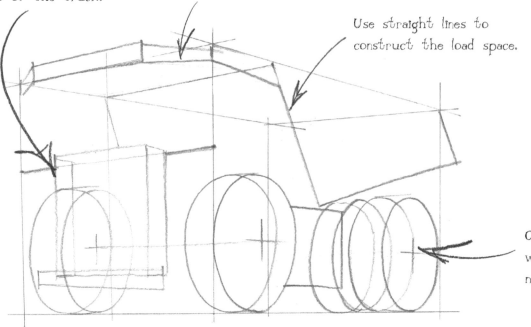

Use straight lines to draw in the area that overhangs the cab.

Add a box to the front of the truck.

Use straight lines to construct the load space.

Construct the wheels with more ellipses.

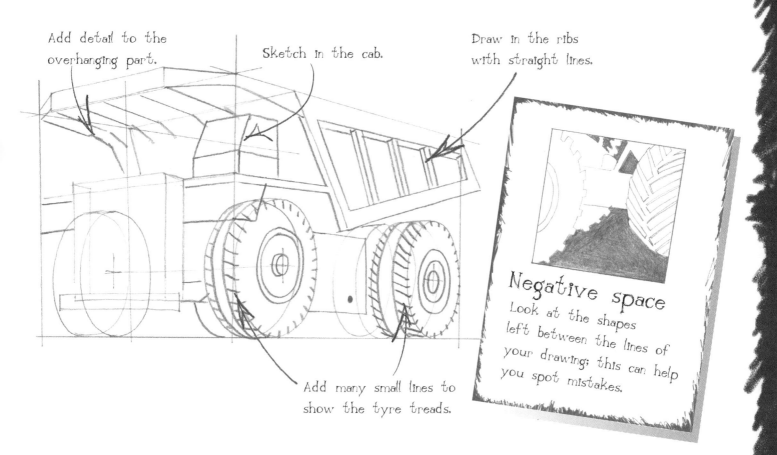

Add detail to the overhanging part.

Sketch in the cab.

Draw in the ribs with straight lines.

Add many small lines to show the tyre treads.

Negative space

Look at the shapes left between the lines of your drawing; this can help you spot mistakes.

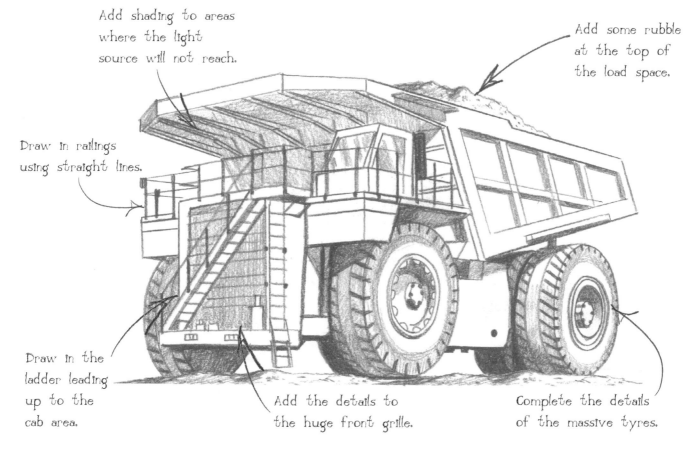

Add shading to areas where the light source will not reach.

Add some rubble at the top of the load space.

Draw in railings using straight lines.

Draw in the ladder leading up to the cab area.

Add the details to the huge front grille.

Complete the details of the massive tyres.

29

Monster truck

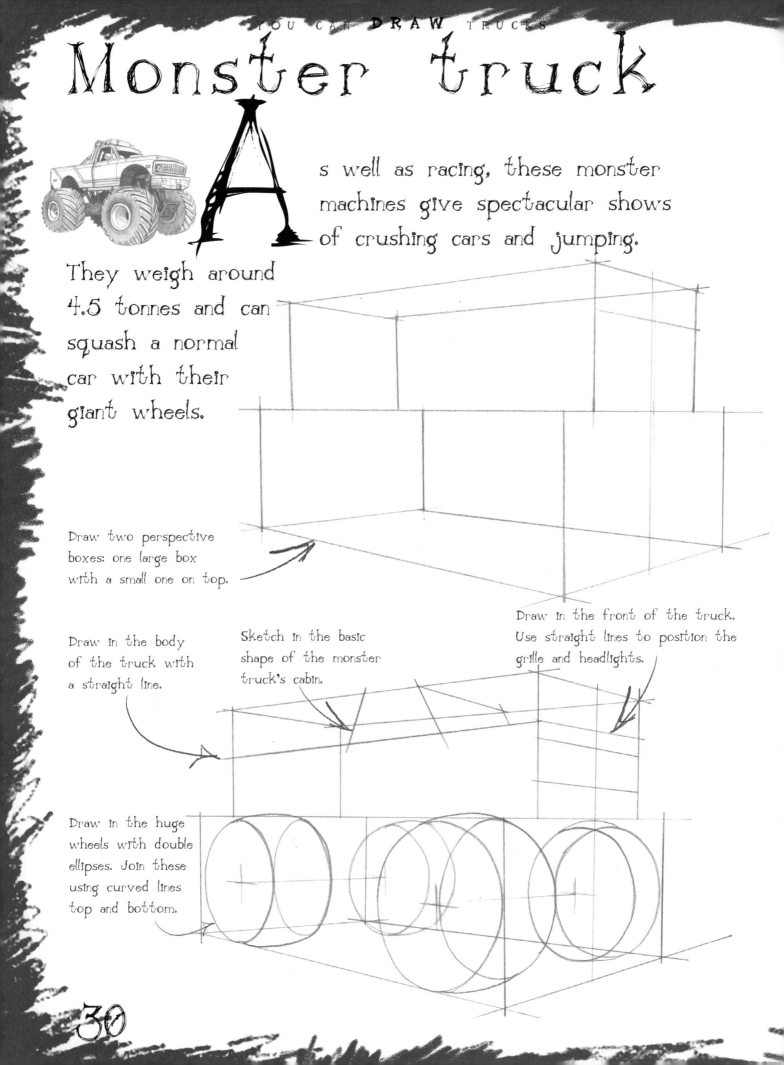

As well as racing, these monster machines give spectacular shows of crushing cars and jumping.

They weigh around 4.5 tonnes and can squash a normal car with their giant wheels.

Draw two perspective boxes: one large box with a small one on top.

Draw in the front of the truck. Use straight lines to position the grille and headlights.

Draw in the body of the truck with a straight line.

Sketch in the basic shape of the monster truck's cabin.

Draw in the huge wheels with double ellipses. Join these using curved lines top and bottom.

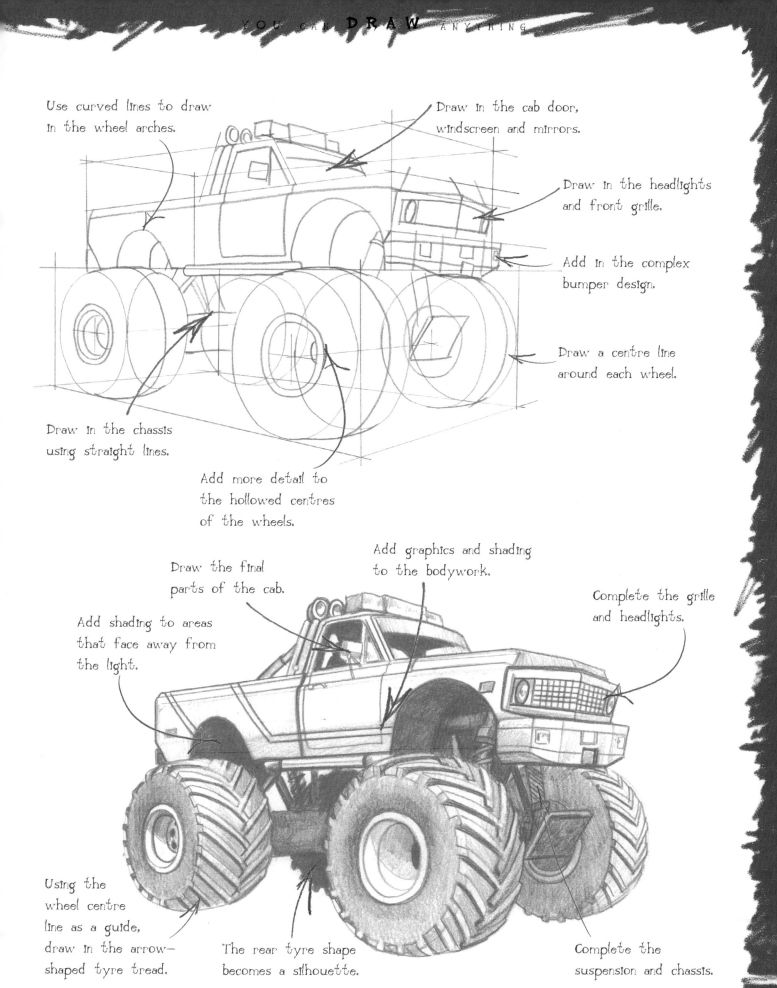

Use curved lines to draw in the wheel arches.

Draw in the cab door, windscreen and mirrors.

Draw in the headlights and front grille.

Add in the complex bumper design.

Draw a centre line around each wheel.

Draw in the chassis using straight lines.

Add more detail to the hollowed centres of the wheels.

Draw the final parts of the cab.

Add graphics and shading to the bodywork.

Complete the grille and headlights.

Add shading to areas that face away from the light.

Using the wheel centre line as a guide, draw in the arrow-shaped tyre tread.

The rear tyre shape becomes a silhouette.

Complete the suspension and chassis.

31

Glossary

Composition The arrangement of the parts of a picture on the drawing paper.

Construction lines Guidelines used in the early stages of a drawing, and usually erased later.

Ellipse An oval shape. When you look at a circle from a position a little to one side, rather than straight on, the shape you see is an ellipse.

Fixative A type of resin used to spray over a finished drawing to prevent smudging. It should only be used by an adult.

Light source The direction from which the light seems to come in a drawing.

Negative space The space around and between the parts of a drawing.

Perspective A method of drawing in which near objects are shown larger than faraway objects to give an impression of depth.

Proportion The correct relationship of scale between each part of the drawing.

Silhouette A drawing that shows only a dark shape, like a shadow.

Squaring up Enlarging a drawing accurately using square grids.

Three-dimensional Having an effect of depth, so as to look lifelike or real.

Vanishing point The place in a perspective drawing where parallel lines appear to meet.

Index

A
articulated truck 18–19

B
backgrounds 9

C
charcoal 10
composition 8, 21
construction lines 15, 16–17, 19, 21, 23, 25, 26–27
crayons 10

D
drawing materials 10–11

E
ellipses 16, 18, 22, 24, 26, 28, 30
exhaust pipes 19, 23
eye level 6–7

F
felt-tips 11
fire engine 16–17
fixative 10
future truck 26–27

G
giant dump truck 28–29

H
headlights 17, 19, 21, 23, 25, 27, 31

I
ink 11

L
light and shade 14–15, 17, 19, 21, 23, 25, 27, 29, 31

M
materials 10–11
mirrors 22
monster truck 30–31

N
negative space 29

P
pastels 10
pencils 10
pens 10
perspective 6–7, 16, 18, 22, 26, 28, 30

R
racing truck 20–21

S
silhouette 10, 31
simple views 14–15
sketching 12–13

T
tanker 24–25

V
vanishing points 6–7